To Jonathan

God Bless
YS

WORDS
OF A MAN
my right to be

Yusef Salaam

WORDS of a Man
my right to be
© 2017 by Yusef Salaam

ISBN 978-0-9796930-2-1

No part of this work may be reproduced in any form without written permission from the author.

Yusef Salaam
Yusef Speaks, LLC
www.yusefspeaks.com : Website
yusef@yusefspeaks.com : Email

Cover photo: Zax Buzz
Background lettering and art by Yusef Salaam
Published by Omo Misha Creative Services
Printed by Lulu Press, Inc.
Manufactured in the United States of America

This book is dedicated to my children:

*Nahtique
Dimani
Rain
Winter
Aaliyah
Poetry
Onaya
Ameerah
Assata
Yusef Amir*

ACKNOWLEDGMENTS
Yusef Salaam

There are so many people I'd like to thank, from my past, present, and future. Everyone I have ever encountered played a small role in the culmination of **"Words of a Man, my right to be"**.

I would like to thank and acknowledge first, The Creator of all things, for providing me this work to do and the wherewithal to do it. A very special thanks and appreciation goes out to my wife Sanovia and our blended family (in order): Nahtique, Dimani, Rain, Winter, Aaliyah, Poetry, Onaya, Ameerah, Assata, and baby Yusef Amir. Thank you for being patient with me and for being my sounding board to this work and works yet to be published.

An extra special thanks to my family, starting with my mother, Sharonne Salaam, for her tirelessness and tenacity in boldly making sure the world never forgot *"Yusef is Innocent"*; and for being my rock and compass in times of darkness and light. To my sister, Aisha, for listening to much of my early work and encouraging me to continue on; always believing in me. To my brother, Shareef, for his constant guidance and encouragement to dream bigger and plan better. He taught me to first to begin with the end in mind and mastermind your plan by working backwards from a finished product to where you currently are. To my Grandmother for encouraging me to be still and listen and for constantly reminding me that I am a master. To my Aunts and Uncles for standing by my side, always believing me and in me. To my Cousin Frank for his guidance, image, encouragement and example to Be Great.

Thank you also to a condensed list of my spiritual family, Imam El-Hajj Talib Abdur Rashid, Sheikh Nuh, Luqman, Abdur-Rasheed (the Lion), Abdul Hakeem, Alim Tajudeen, Muhammad Ali, Sheikh Ahmad Moait, a special thanks goes out to Brother

Jerome Jones for being the spark by asking me The question… *"**Who are you?**"* allowing me to begin the process of becoming what I was to become.

And a very special thanks goes to my good friend Omo Misha for guiding me through the self-publishing process, and assisting me with designing this book.

I am genuinely appreciative for everyone who played even the smallest role in the creation, enhancement, or promotion of this work. Thank You!!!!! Thank You!!! Thank You!

Sharing the struggle,

Yusef

FOREWORD
Sharonne Salaam

    I never would have thought I'd be here today; but this life is not about me. It's about a fifteen year-old boy who through all odds was able to hold onto life after false arrest, living behind bars, walking beside hate, racism and discrimination. It's all about my son Yusef Salaam.

    Yusef always talked about how poetry helped him hold it together. Here in his first collection he shares some of his poems with the world. Hoping that they could help people in their time of despair to know there is a way if they just hold on.

Yusef spent seven years in jail, followed by three years on parole and was on Megan's List as a sexual predator. He was hated in the community by many and loved by few. This experience
lasted thirteen years until a miracle happened. Matias Reyes, a serial rapist and murderer, already in jail, confessed to the crime. And, low and behold, his story of events of that night and his DNA matched for the first time.

    Even today, in many circles, Yusef and the other boys are still spoken of and treated as if they
were guilty. Not as the innocent, wrongfully incarcerated and exonerated men they are today.

    It's been over twenty-five years and none of the police who participated in this travesty of justice were ever held accountable for their actions.

    Now a man, Yusef holds onto forgiveness as he speaks, writes, and touches people with his heart.

Sharonne Salaam

INTRO
Yusef Salaam

When I initially started writing it was because, like many young brothers, I wanted to be a hip-hop artist. I had been writing rhymes since I was eleven or twelve years old. The Central Park Five case happened in 1989, during an era in music where message-style hip-hop songs were hot. *Self Destruction,* KRS-One's *Love's Gonna Get'cha*, and especially Public Enemy were some of the artists and songs that were shaping my style as a writer, and were essentially the soundtrack of my life. I especially gravitated toward Public Enemy, who came out with a flow that listened less like rap, and more like a speech. When I got convicted, it was the beginning of me realizing that I needed to say something. "How am I going to say something?", I wondered. "How am I going to stand for myself, and what am I going to use?" For the first time, I realized that this art-form I had been honing from childhood, that had been gathered and polished from all I had seen and experienced in my short time on earth, was going to allow me to get my message across at this most critical point in my life.

> "How am I going to say **something...**How am I going to stand for myself & what am I going to **use?**"

Looking back on the day I was convicted, I remember being in and out of the courtroom. I had my shades on, head up, trying to feel and look confident; trying to be strong in the face of a very serious situation. At the same time, and still after everything we had already been through, I'd held out hope that the system would not fail us – that justice would prevail. If you look back on the footage from that day, what you will see is a young man who was sure he was going home that day. When the verdict came down and we were convicted, I was completely devastated. Never in a million years could you have convinced me that the system was going to do us like this, and then...the system did us like that.

Now, here I was in the courthouse, waiting for my sentence and being told that I should throw myself on the mercy of the court; that I should plead for the least amount of time possible. But, I had been reading about Malcolm X and others who were in the struggle; I had been inspired by hip-hop acts who were using their art to spread powerful messages about our experiences, and I started writing instead. The words literally flowed through me, like I was a vessel. And, when our sentences were handed down and I was given the stage to say my piece, I read *I Stand Accused*. It had been penned in that moment, and summed up everything I felt and knew I needed to say, to the court and to the world.

As time passed, not only was art something that allowed me to escape the harsh realities of imprisonment, but being able to write about these experiences was tremendous in that it, really, saved my life. Being able to share my thoughts on paper, especially in an artistic way gave me an out. It provided a relief that I couldn't find in any other way. My mother used to always say to me that everybody – everybody – has gifts and that these gifts are the way to freedom. She would say that I was blessed with a bunch of different types of gifts. I didn't always understand what she meant by that but I knew that she was trying to encourage me and make me see things in a positive light. But, I have since learned to see, embrace, and even build on those gifts – drawing, writing poetry and rhymes...I've even learned to speak. I was 15,16 years old when my reality changed forever. This situation that you would think would be so debilitating actually allowed me to find the strength and the power, not only to help myself but to also to help others. I never thought about being a source of power or strength for another person, just by them seeing me stand up, or hearing me talk about things. In many ways, the rest of the world doesn't know that I write poetry, so in a way this is my way of revealing that part of myself to the world as well; letting them know that Yusef is a multi-faceted, complicated individual who's ready to take his position in life.

Most of the poetry in this book was written while I was incarcerated (1989-1997). There are pieces that were written after that, but the bulk of the material took shape while I was in prison. I've always called this body of work *Words of a Man* because the social and justice systems weren't treating me like a man: From the unbelievable accusation from the start; to the wild convictions of the media; to Donald Trump's full page ad calling for the State to kill us; to the final judgment and imprisonment. The system was not treating me as if I was a man, so because I knew I was a man – a human being, a son of Allah – I had to remind myself, and these words were a big part of that. Here I was at the beginning of this whole bid, and I had to grow up very, very fast. But, I wanted to share this work specifically because I wanted people to know that when you find yourself in *so-called* dark places, there's always a light somewhere in the darkness, and even if that light is inside of you, you can illuminate your own darkness by shedding that light on the world.

Power Post: Because the world must know.

Yusef Salaam

CONTENTS

- My Mother 1
- Live 2
- POETRY 3
- Blank Canvas 4
- Life is Grand 5
- The Puzzle 6
- The World 8
- Unfaithful 9
- Stopping by the Road on a Windy Day 10
- Them 12
- Truth 13
- New York-ish 14
- Heartbeat 15
- Reverse the Curse 16
- Who are you 17
- Today I Celebrate You 18
- Dream State 19
- Words of a Man 20
- I used to be a slave 21
- Message to Mankind 22
- A heart's wet secret 24
- The One 25
- Things I didn't know I Loved 26
- The Revolution will not be televised 27
- Colored 28
- Blue Feather 29
- Ladybug 30
- Willow Tree 31

- Waves.. 32
- Am I Black Enough for You........................ 33
- War.. 34
- Sometimes... 35
- I Need You... 36
- Mine... 38
- More Man.. 39
- The Silent Majority.................................... 40
- Captivity... 41
- Sleep in Unity.. 42
- Harlem... 43
- Blood... 44
- I'll Meet You Between Venus & Mars............. 45
- Trickier than Bewitched............................. 46
- Malcolm.. 47
- Darkie.. 48
- Animals.. 49
- Educate a Man.. 50
- Legal Lynching.. 51
- JUSTICE... 52
- Sweet Lady... 53
- A Bear Named Alfalfa............................... 54
- Honey Wine.. 56
- Good Cop, Bad Cop................................. 57
- I smell a rat.. 58
- I Stand Accused...................................... 61
- One 9 eight 9: the turning point................. 64
- What Happens to a Justice Delayed........... 65
- This Racist Death Penalty......................... 66
- Freestylin'.. 67

WORDS
OF A MAN
my right to be

Yusef Salaam

My Mother

1

Bold

Beautiful

Beloved

Black

Divine

Loving

Mother

Shero

Warrior

Queen

2 Live

Do you think we are afraid to die
Wallahi we not afraid to live
Every one dies
Not all of us lives
My God
I have my soul to give

POETRY   3

Picking pineapples by the sea
Oranges, cantaloupe, grapes; oh wee
Every fruit I love to eat
Tangerines a special treat
Red strawberries ripe and sweet
Yellow starfish what to eat?
Mangos, grapefruits let me think…

I think I'll have a banana

4 — Blank Canvas

Each of us are born into this world like a blank canvas
And everyone that comes across our path
leaves a mark on our surface
And thus we grow
But there comes a time
we have to pick up our own brush
and determine who and what we'll be
Just another painting
or a masterpiece

As told to me by Brother Shabaka Alkebulan
while were both at Clinton Dannemora prison

Life is grand

Anyway
Life is grand
Standing in a sea of flowers
a life-sized kaleidoscope
Sending natural peaceful auras through me
Nature is me
This is where I want to be
below the sky
slowly
swaying in the wind
catching the rays
letting the haze add to the mystical
more better sea
near the great pine
by the edge of the stone wall
a big, bold, barrier
the only sign that says man was here.

6 The Puzzle

I took out a pen
and wrote another line
a page in time
a note
another rhyme...
some did ask why was the beat so smooth
lyrics flow slow to enhance the mood
got the people dancing and shorty is whipped
I stop and take a pause and put the mike on my hip
I'm smooth my rhymes are somewhat subtle
I snatch the mike up and add a piece to the puzzle
Rhymes that's made to rock
style gallant
so I'm a flaunt this
Style that I bring to make you sing
and make you want it
flourish and flourish and flourish and flourish then flow
Fee die foe, Yo! discover the reel
spinning I flow smooth at ease
Evolve to 180 Degrees if Allah please
My heart is open if knowledge is sought
is not the lessons the knowledge of the mis-taught

Yusef Salaam

I rise from the dead through a path there's Heaven
I sport more skills than double 0 seven
Cut it out, you're not messing with this lesson
Because the sight of the Smith and Wesson,
won't leave a question
The sight of sleek swine slight flicked with wine
Refined with worm lines
Peace! It's time.
The Puzzle

8 — The World

The world will have you on some La Lillahah ish
And make you forget that ill LaAllah bit
You run your program and crash your ish
cause of that missing bit
Producing all errors and ish.

Unfaithful

Her mood changes like the wind
She's unfaithful in the summer
If I would have known it then
I'd refuse to be her lover

Stopping by the road on a windy day

10

(A mixture of strong wind and damaging rain bore down on that small town)

boooooommmmmmmmmmm!!!!!!!!!!!!!!!!

They say lightning never strikes twice
this was the exception

not five seconds after the car was brought
to an inevitable halt
the tree was struck a second time
continuing the jagged electric cut through the other half of the great oak

In what seemed to be a time
without dimension
the thick tree sliced through the air
smooth
like a stone being tossed on a windless day
smashing the steel capsule below
the impact shattered each of the six windows
one
by one
a fraction of a second after the other

Then things happened in freeze frames without sound

Yusef Salaam

he lifted hand severed in two as the avalanched tree impacted causing the metal to cave creating a perfectly serrated edge

his thumb caressed the breeze gently as it lulled him to sleep

Deeper

as part of the dashboard cut into fiber / then flesh / then bone releasing the feeling of his toes on the smoked black floor mat

and then nothing

Them

Racists aim at blacks to take them
Down the road with nooses - hang them
I cross downtown streets to shake them
Like I'm on the court pump - fake them
Abusers of the rules - all day them
Complexion for protection - they them
Planned annihilation - slay them
Silent screams of hatred - they them
Kill them all today - us who them
Place no tag on toe - the nerve them
Potter's field with hoes we destine
Awake us today - who us them
Reconstruct our play - we know them
Now from checkers - chess we play them
Mastering the game - we made them
Bopping from the whip - we slay them

Truth

Days at a time
Where has it gone
Sitting in my cell singing a sad song
Bars on the window
I'm locked away
No one seems to care today

I want justice to give back
What has been taken from us
So many are willing to freely give
What we're fighting to gain

14 — New York-ish

New York will have you on some
eat a cat like a lion
Spit the bones out
and beat they soul with it

Heartbeat

We are at war
The bulk of which will not be physical
The bulk of which is mental
Psychological warfare
To make me accept you as better
Like your ice is cooler or water, wetter
Holding court in the streets
This time court will be sweet
We will not accept defeat
The signal will be your heartbeat.

16 Reverse the Curse

We have the power to fight
We have the power to win
We have the power to love and support each other
We have nothing to lose but our chains

("It is our duty to fight for our freedom.
It is our duty to win.
We must love each other and support each other.
We have nothing to lose but our chains."
- Assata Shakur)

He fell first
Threw him off the building head first
Body all mangled couldn't fit in a hearse
They caused me to reverse the curse
We gon' die so reverse the curse
Body all mangled couldn't fit in a hearse
Throw 'em off the building head first

Who are you — 17

Searching to find **who** has come
A beautiful **soul** a powerful one

Today I Celebrate You

Today I celebrate you
For without you they would not be
Our history
Allows their existence to see
And our ending, means our beginning times 3
Like *"if I could find a spot where truth echoes*
I'd go there and Whisper memories of our children's future"
Through God, I found the greatest suitor

To Him I offer praise
And thanks for this divine day
With your coming
This day is marked as greatness day

Happy birthday to you
And many more
Our future is brightened
With three great stars

Dream State

Green haze colored my Dream state
Anything
Everything
Held this trait
The dome in its brilliance held it too
Reminding me of places I've never been
See only in an eastern wind
Sins scent
Is bent
Because the dome is sacred
Memorizing
Internalizing
Real subduing fake
Naked nests are clearly seen
Down
And
Up
The hill to the beginning
Returning to the dome through a glance
Never to erase this permanent stamp

20 Words of a Man

I am a Blackman

A dead man walking

Death comes before my time

Because of sick minds

Hell bent evil intent

At the helm of the death ship

Shipping us in boxes to the earth

Throwing dirt on my birth

I am the last so

I am the first

I am a Blackman

a Blackman walking

I used to be a slave — 21

I used to be a slave

Till I freed

I used to be a slave

Because of your greed

Message to Mankind

Brother step unto me like yo! Who you be?
I be a man of Islam Yusef on the scene
The knowledge of Islam puts you back on the right track
Cause messing with the devil means you're picking up slack
The wicked I kill
Heads I break at will
Cool, calm at first then I show my skill
This is a message to those who won't believe
Weak minded brothers that can't perceive
The devil only has power over that which you give it
Righteous my life so that's how I'm living
Back in the days I'd be a field nigger not an Uncle Tom
Man in charge, I drop bombs
What in hell makes you think I'ma fall off
When under my trench there's a fist like a sawed off
I'm hitting hard like a bullet
Demolishing negative-ness I'ma pull it
Back, strong then release
In your ass was a black bad beast

I spoke with words like steel
Feeling strong so I speak what I feel
On the stage lyrics are ignited
You know it's hype, you can't fight it
Have you forgotten we were brought to this land
We were robbed of our language I can't understand

Yusef Salaam

How they could just take our language away
And leave us sitting on the side without much to say
Cool as a night breeze I step forth
Stronger and longer, I'ma come off
Here's the wisdom of a wise spoken Blackman
Yo! Knowledge is at hand
Yes they call me knowledge I'm a higher breed
I spread knowledge around the world as I plant the seed
Like Malcolm I give knowledge to the young
Cause I know where the Blackman is coming from
And where we're going as we step forth
As you can see we retreated to the north
Movement of the people as Bob Marley said
The flame of the youth is this torch at hand

My words uplift
And bring a gift that's swift
The knowledge combined with this style as you're taking a sip
Take a seat knowledge is at hand

I'ma man of Islam the supreme
The name Allah, strong like a steel beam
Keep calm, situation underhand
All Afrikan mixed with native land
International went the words I speak
Be on your guard like a cop on the street
In Sha Allah you'll be back on the plane
Don't fall asleep, don't let the devil take your brain
International went the words I speak
See you later, once again peace!!!

24 — A heart's wet secret

I hear the soft wet drops as they land on the windowpane
I hear the secret voice as it whispers out your name
I see two people walking embraced in each other's arms
Through the dewy grass
The aftermath
Of a late night storm
I feel the magnetic force as it draws me closer to you
I feel the romantic vibes, in the light breeze that cool night blew
Quivering emotions rise and fall inside of me
The two people I see embraced in each other's arms are you and me
I feel loved, the kind of love you wake up to
Like soft sweet loving music that puts you in the mood
A moment like this is needed for all and is a blessing from above
A heart's wet secret is best described as you and I making love

The One

In the name of Allah because Allah's names are grand
Not for the jams my man but take a stand and
Give respect when respect due is given
Allah the Self-Sufficient
Absolute
The Ever-Living
He the Eternal without beginning or end
Allowed me to convey the word through the form of a pen
Be and it is, how the command was released
And if all would join together in Unity
Just to know Allah is the Master of all
With Him you best believe your 'bout twelve feet tall
Feeling strong like a walk that's made of stone
Allah gives me strength so I can hold my own
Ain't giving it up so turn me loose
You want juice, profess the truth.

Things I didn't know I loved

I didn't know I loved to read
Open my mind
Feel a breeze
Thinking about home...
I didn't know I loved being free
Walking the streets
Feeling sweet

I saw my girl the other day
I didn't know I loved to play
Feeling gay...but not that way

I didn't know I loved to travel
See new things, meet other beings

I didn't know I loved the quiet
Unlike the riots
The things that I grew used to

I didn't know that I loved peace.

The Revolution Will Not Be Televised

I can remember when that statement made me sad inside
Too young to be in it
Now I couldn't even see it, Why?
why couldn't the revolution be televised?
The Last Poets'
Gil Scott Heron
As I grew up I began to see
They left theirs and I too wanted to leave a mark on History
A Man in half and I wanted to bask
in the task that set men free
But a revolution
The Revolution, is where I knew I had to be
The Revolution will not be televised
They don't want to display the victory of those "Lesser Men"
The Revolution will not be televised
Smile I know
Because I am the evolution of the Revolution!

Colored

They say we're colored
They are like prism
Cause we have the melanin
They want us to give them
They turn blue when dead
Red in the head when cold
Frost sneaks up bold

Blue Feather

A blue feather falling in the wind
Falls slow but floats with the wind
Enters your mind like a pull of a sess blunt
Visions of paradise with a sharp edge that's blunt
Mysteries that set themselves in a grave
Death awaits us all, therefore be not to this life a slave
Make your decisions and move on slow
But shit is real so why not move fast
Thinking means you won't last,
instinct saves the ass
You have to instinct in the concrete jungle,
to strive, to survive
Just do what you have to,
do to others as others do to you
When I get bent, I must represent no question
Get up a dime spot,
then I off to the dread section
Purity represents the truth and I be
A blue feather fallin' in the wind.

Ladybug

The lady bug Flies

Up,

    Down

        Spinning

                        No control

In tornado winds

Willow Tree — 31

The willow tree in
The morning, cascading
On the horizon.

Waves

You could hear the waves

Rolling in against the shore,

Inducing my sleep.

Am I Black Enough for You

I woke up this morning
Ate a bowl of Cheerios and Wheaties.
Am I black enough for you?

Walking around
Turning your head,
Dyeing your hair
Bleaching your underwear,
Putting your nose up in the air.
Black mocha, yellow, green, chocolate sugar
I love you more than you love yourself.
Am I black enough for you?

I want to support you and protect you
I want to respect you and love you
I want to kiss you and hold you all through the night
I want to make your life turn out right.

I am putting my cards on the table.
I am in for the long hall.
Am I black enough for you?

Goddess of the world speak to me
No matter what color you be.
You are not alone, we are together you see.
I am here to do my part for you and the children too.

Am I black enough for you?

Make a place for me at your table. I am ready!
I am ready!!
I am ready!!!
Am I black enough for you?
Am I black enough?
Am I?

34 — War

I beat my chest to check my vest

Sometimes

Sometimes
I think and wonder about things we do
About how you've got a man
And how much I love you

Sometimes
When I kiss your cheeks
When I kiss your lips
It's like two souls meeting

Sometimes
Every time
I see you it's like the first time
Please take this moment to say that you'll be mine

I Need You

When you hold me in your arms
And cuddle me near
Your touch is like a breeze
A whisper in the night
That it puts me at ease

My one and only love
Like a lost treasure
You are the one I seek

The time we've spent together
The love that I've learned
No more fun and games for me
You know how my heart burns

I wake up in a sweat
I need your caress
That tender loving care
I can get from no one else

I ask to touch you
Your answer is yes

Then I kiss your cheek
It's you that I need

Your body is warm
It prepares the perfect mood
As I think of a poem

Yusef Salaam

To be
Or not to be
No that's not the one
Let's get it on
Boldly I move turning of the light
Our bodies in motion
The moment is right

Smooth as I lay you on bed sheets
You know what I need
Cool I say kissing you
Our bodies touch
Your body flutters like a bird
In my hand

Please take this moment
To say that you need me too
Because you are for me
Because I need you

Mine

Muscles flexed
Body arched
After a hard day's work
Please say you'll be mine
Or my feelings will be hurt

More Man

To be more than a man
But not degrading the man
Like living in the jungle
Watch for quick sand
Trained to trick

Sometimes beasts take human form
Caught in a raid like roaches running from Raid
It puts a frown on your face
To see how many people accept the subject
Why should we be oppressed?
We get no respect?
They say whites are king,
King rules pawn, pawn is we
This story is all wrong
There are no jobs for the poor
They throw our youth in the sack
But this is my way to get back

The Silent Majority

Material things
Selling drugs for gold colors
Flipping has me turning against my brother
The unwise are at the mercy of the wise
They did not realize it
Until a family member died

Now tell me why
You want to be in the belly of the beast
A dumb man sings a dead man song
The devil's advocate is trying
To teach the youth wrong

In the street a mother weeps
Sign of the times
This is getting deep
Hold on
I want to teach
The each
To know right from wrong

I used to write rhymes just for fun
But now
I write to be the one
The one among many whom has learned
Learned the trade
And put their mind in place
To unleash their rage

Captivity

Stop killing brother
You are all ready marked
Because of your color
So why not put our youth in jail
Chance they will become like snails
Chance they won't rebel

On me they left indelible scars
There was a time I talked behind bars
They thought that this would get me
Like Kunta in captivity
I am still free

Up north I come from down south
With the greatest tool of man
His mouth
Whether dark as mud
Or tan as sand
Dark in color is the dapperest Dan

Talking about history
Too to many young folks
Living in mystery

Things I have read
Talked about blood shed
And of the dead
Neither hurt my ears
Nor left my eyes in tears

I overcame fears
Not afraid to take a chance
Cause pain grips my heart
As I look to the mother land
I am here in captivity
Who is more free you or me

Sleep In Unity

If we stay asleep
We can't get back the time
Like a guy on a trip
Without a road map
I was taught to help the sisters
And the brothers
If you know the way
Why not light it for the others
Sometimes you see me chilling
Riding by in a car
Now I educate sisters and brothers
Don't perpetuate stars
This is the answer
To many of our people
I see dying like cancer
What is wrong with unity?
Bringing people together
Exerts the pure beauty of unity.

Harlem

Harlem

Much chaos

Glocks lock the block

A brownstone on 141st street

Police coming in hot

A little boy plays with a rubber duck

Pop pop pop

In a warm tub

Another one drops.

Blood

Black bodies turned against each other
Lost in the world
Thinking its about money and girls
Light up in the Bronx,
the tenements look pretty now
Colors of bright orange, red and blue
Over a cloud of thick dust and unbearable heat
Onyx eyes, beautiful and bright sit in a corner
In a body trembling, rag cloaked.

I'll Meet You Between Venus & Mars

In between Venus and Mars

Is the center of our attraction

Of those connected to the stars

Hardly a fraction

It behooves man to work for the day

when this will all end

Life is mortal, so follow the way of those heaven sent

Awaken and receive that which will give you life

Or remain horizontal and never begin the flight

For the solution, I'll descend from amongst the stars

And I'll meet you between Venus and Mars.

Trickier Than Bewitched

Will we ever figure this out...
Shackling the mind with our consent
Bent, from the natural order of this universe.
Shackling the mind with our consent?
What do you see when you see me?
The enemy,
The inner me?
How did they trick the un-trick able ones?
How did they bewitch the natural mystics?
I'll tell you!
I'll tell you!!!
I'd tell you of a time when I looked back
The lash on my back
The axe on my feet,
Making it unable for me to walk straight.
And with my mouth agape, I
I vibrate, instead of scream
No longer cry...
Wishing to die

My tongue is gone, last seen on the sand,
near the shores
of this strange land
My eyes lie (synonym for next to them)
How did they trick the un-trick-able ones?
How did they bewitch the natural mystics?
I'll tell you!
I'll tell you!!!
It was sick!

Malcolm

Malcolm
You labeled him a militant
You failed to understand
About the great man

The American dream is a myth
If one obtains power like his
You get death

We still fall deep
As we climb to the top
The mountain gets steep
Unlike Malcolm we are to afraid to try
Why-oh-why do you let the race die?

Malcolm
You labeled him a militant
He tried to show you the way
All he got was a bullet
And not even a holiday.

48 Darkie

Threatened by neighbors
And feared by white America
They say you can't see a black man at night
Dark and proud I'll fight for what is right
Say it loud, louder, loudest
Darkie this is the hour.

Animals

They labeled us animals
But failed to understand
We knew they were cannibals
In the Promise Land

They hide the truth
So I let it loose
Giving knowledge to youth

The duck of the world was heard
To most this was what we were referred
But we are not ducks or slaves or such
We've long since
Stopped saying
Yes sa,
Masa.

Educate A Man

Before there was any history
There was OUR history
This is not a game book puzzle like mystery

His-story is dead
Stop talking the lies
We've been freed
Pick up a book and read

Before there was any history
There was OUR history
This is not a game book puzzle like mystery

His-story is dead
Stop talking in lies
We free
Pick up a book and read
Yeah I used to hate
What I used to need.

Legal Lynching

Six boys, accused of the same crime,
They're innocent and the truth will come out in time.
Six boys, Just Playin' in the Park,
Unaware of the dangers in the dark,
Six boys, going to court every day,
Six mothers, all they can do is sit and pray……..

Its legal lynchin'
No concern with the truth.
Legal Lynchin'
Come to take away our youth
Legal Lynchin'
No more hangin from the tree
Legal Lynchin'
Could happen to you, Happened to me.

An evil judge got his job with a bribe,
The prosecutor wants to win to save her pride.
A sick press convinced the people of the lie,
Defense attorneys too afraid to even try.

It's Legal Lynchin'
Not concerned with D.N.A
Legal Lynchin'
That's the weapon of today
Legal Lynchin'
No presumption of innocence
Legal Lynchin'
Not concerned with evidence
Legal Lynchin'
        Lord, it doesn't make much sense.

Legal Lynching was a gift from Ayesha Grice.
She shared the piece with reporters after the first trial –
where Anton, Raymond, and I were convicted and
locked away as we awaited sentencing.

JUSTICE

Saying down with the black
Uplift the white
Justice, unjust
Black robes pale face
Black robe black face
Black robe no face
Justice, unjust
Justice
Just
Us.

Sweet Lady

I can make you feel like a butterfly
when you are near
And make you feel like a rainbow
    When the skies in your sight are unclear
Because I feel like a flower
growing in your great garden
Nice to be a part of you
    Your heart is what I'll win
You'll feel like ears
    Hearing the master piece of great sound
Redefined to peace
    You'll be my Queen, so humbly accept this crown
You know…
     I feel like a fish, swimming in a great sea
But I'd feel much, much, better
  If you felt like me
        My Sweet Lady

A Bear Named Alfalfa
– a short story

A Bear named Alfalfa
    Resting in the woods
        Covered with snow
With its head peaking out of an opening
Peacefully...sound asleep
Like a king NO ONE DARE DISTURB
As I stop to catch a glimpse of this wonderful sight
I am reminded of great sculptors
engraving their work
    Into solid slates of ice.
His beard is shaped like an upside-down icicle ...as if frozen,
flowing water
The drops on his fur seem to just sit there
    Timeless
A single drop on an artist's page

Ah, the wind...
As the breeze sails by
I inhale fresh, cool nostril opening air
Almost too cool to breathe
Walking closer
    I breathe the sound of nothing

        And stoop near Alfalfa to touch the snow
I am flung far from there
        Now at the end of a fresh trail of blood
                Gushing from my wound
Alas, I look to see Alfalfa lying down
Back into his casing
        An impression of snow
                His winter coffin

…Back to his hibernation.

Honey Wine

This is for the lady
    Whose kiss is sweeter than honey wine
With deep rich complexion
    That's so sublime
Face of an angel
    Body like an hour glass
Around my heart
    You've gently tied your sash
In your walk is a dance
In your stride you prance
Tantalizing   me
    Forever
        You
            I'll romance
We'll sit in the warmth
With the fire ablaze
You in my arms
    The tender loving phase
With all I've said
    I must also say
I wish you a beautiful birthday
    On this happy day.

Good Cop, Bad Cop

They've come in to coax you

Trickery, don't refuse
"Come, down to the station"
They catch you while you snooze
Once downstairs you're surrounded
by the criminal dressed in blue
Faces I dread, dead faces
     They catch you while you snooze
"Come downstairs…an echo" but you go anyway
In their house you're surrounded,
and you don't know their game…

"Muther fu@#*%..."they confront you
Trying to knock you out your space
The other, calm, fake protect you
And you…falling their prey
Without knowing, you've sold your soul,
in this house of deceit
You were all too innocent,
now in this beast belly you weep.

58 — I smell a rat

"The scene opens up to a woman. The camera zooms in on her...her closer...her womb, and then it goes through her...to her mother...her mother's mother...and so on and so on and so on..."

I bet you didn't see me when I was behind the bush,
You tried to tax (slang: take) that but you just couldn't push
Your twig, it's a sprinkle of the black man's middle
Check the repartee' as I unfold this riddle
Back in the days I had a kingdom that was great
Then you tried to come and take my moms on a date
She didn't want to go
So you dragged her down slow
My pops would have bussed you in the head,
but he didn't know
Overwhelmed by the promise of a better life west
Didn't know the promise excluded him and the rest
Didn't smell the rat until it was too late
The ones (who) refused, hung in nooses
while the rest was chained
but a chain is only as strong as its weakest link
Stop! The missing link, is what you seek, don't blink
Blink again and I'm gone like the wind
in' sha-Allah, I'll return 4 centuries from then.

Roughly 400 years later
Catch it on your beta
Another black child is born

To this scorn
Near the equator
Muslim, second born,
my pop's and mom's divorced
The absence of him, was the absence of the source
I sink into the link, is what I seek...to the 60's nah, even before, when things wasn't so nifty.
I wish I was there to meet the man,
be the man, he the man...
He taught me to check the conspiracy
To see what's there to see
But they caught me
In other words...
I realized the experiment
Before I got enthralled with the local events
Sprayed with a chemical
That blurred my subliminal
They had me thinking like a criminal
I became analytical
And dissected the devil
I read my mind to another level
(Read about them...) licking on the bearer of fruit
They say the blacker the berry
The sweeter the juice
So keep your eyes on the prize
But realize, that I see clear
Allah got my back I enter in without fear
I won't let them trick me again
Instead I'll ascend and with Allah we win
An intelligent Muslim
And the Ummah of the Muslims are friends.
Jack of all trades, in a deck, I'm the highest spade

You can't out think a thinker that Allah made
You tried to come get me played
but I'm Muslim made
Pull out the gauge
Take the air waves
A man's greatness lies in the power of thought
Can the devil fool a Muslim?
Only if he is lost
Train your heart and soul right enough to be boss
You're not Allah, praise Allah and recognize the source
Uh- silent assassins, they tried to take me like Malcolm
You came with a gun I came with the Wild West
You came with a gun I came with the Wild West
You came with a gun I came with the Wild West (echo x3)
You came with a gun I came with the Wild West
Bulletproof on your chest, not enough to impress, 'cause
Teflon is the type with the hollow point tip
Lettin' you know not to flip, 'cause you can get it
I'm pretty damn sharp
So let's start
You can't escape
Remember the ones you stole,
remember the ones' you raped
Dipped in you like the Big Dipper
Flipped like a flipper
Guide the boat like the skipper
Reverse
And I'll lynch ya' Dirty Rat

I Stand Accused

I'm not going to sit here at your table and watch you eat and call myself dinner. Sitting here at your table doesn't make me dinner just as being in America doesn't make me an American.

~ El-Hajj Malik Shabazz (Malcolm X)!

Let us begin!
Stress, stress is the anger that is built up inside
Rage is the anger that is no longer built
Taken on a sucker, that you're trying to kill
American freewill doesn't mean you can kill
And take another person's life
You live your life trife
I'm a skill builder
So on skills I do build
Creator given knowledge to this wise black man
Soon to enhance
My words across the land

I'm a smooth type of fellow
Cool, calm and mellow
I'm kind of laid back
But now I'm speaking so that you know
I got used
And abused
And even was put on the news
And on cue, they gave clues selling out like fools
Now check this...who did what
And who did who in
You're put in a situation that you don't know what to do and some people go wilding'
We're not down with them
Who would have thought we'd have to lock in

I stand accused
I'm still accused

Checking the scene from how the situation was,
Instead of getting facts the media made you blurred
Now the people don't know,
All they hear is the media
They never hear the blamed
Cause they're constantly deceiving us

D.A. Is dead wrong,
This is her master plan
This case is not a case
It's just a crafter sham

Yo!!!!
Instead of trying to get your name made,
It's reconstructing the crime that really pays.

Islam, la illaha illallah,
Born supreme over shaytan, but no man is Allah.
Yes I'm a science dropper on the righteous path
So how the hell could I take a rapist path?
Think about that and then think about this,
All my friends it was me they dissed
they're dismissed.
I don't really need any friends like that,
Like...
When I really needed you, where were you at?
I'm not dissing them all
But the sum that I called
They went and dissed me,
like I was an inch small
Like a rat, a mouse, not even a man
Wrongly accused, like the knife's in my hand.
How does it look,
Me clocked now I'm shook

Yusef Salaam

But like Matlock, soon the accused gets off the hook.
It's real when she remembers and says,
Nah, it wasn't them, and the cops did you in.

I stand accused
I'm still accused
You people stop...the racial disperse
Aye yo! You seen that kid Benson? He's in a hearse.
And so we take it to the Benson Hurst fields,
Whites have bulletproof vest, and we've got no kind of shields
How does that look they killed a black man,
Being black, it's time to take a stand.
In our situation you saw our faces clear,
But not mine, not because of fear,
It's because the black race was disgraced
As for the Muslims, they must have felt shamed
But I'm not to blame with the words you bought,
The media took their words to paper
The ones the cops distorted
I told the cops truth like this, and then BOOM...!
Man they smacked my man Wise up in the next room.

Now I know why the Rasta's can't stand de Babylon
Dem changing up like decepticons.
I used to think the people and cops were cool...
But who protects us from you...

I stand accused!!!!!!!

Yusef Salaam!
Copyright 1990

Closing remarks, written and recited at the Central Park Five trial, before sentencing.

One 9 eight 9: the turning point

Saying down with the blacks but uplift the white race
Scottsboro, Scapegoats…Six more kismet
Justice unjust, black robes and pale face

Raising the banner to the sun in haste
Mobbed deep, hoods and capes (ref. to the KKK) sun dried,
(stained with blood) after being wet
Saying down with the blacks but uplift the white race

Unjustly tried…an indelible conviction of rape
The usual result of what six shades of darker skin get
Justice unjust black robes and pale face

Didn't have a chance, six youth among apes
I wish I would have known the false smile
…seen the subtle sweat
Saying down with the blacks but uplift the white race

Evil intentions, fulfilling their taste
Why me…us? Losers in this camouflage gauntlet
Justice unjust, black robes and pale face

Black, or shades of brown,
we must keep the pace
Under burdens, pain in our backs,
erase the mindset of…
Saying down with the blacks but uplift the white race,
Justice unjust, black robes and pale face!

What happens to a Justice Delayed?

It is denied. Is that what this is this time?
Time and time again, before…now…and then
Justice delayed…Justice denied.
drying up like a grape in the sun
our indelible scars festering and running.
after a justice delayed too long
eluding us like forgotten words to a song.
We
are
struggling
to put our live back
Resuscitating ourselves before we lie flat.
a life that stank like rotting meat
no roses to smell
not sugary sweet.
Eluding us like it's trying to escape
Unable to erase the label of rape.
I'm pissed as I carry this heavy load…..
I want to explode!!!!!
What happens to a Justice Delayed?

66 — This Racist Death Penalty

They used to have us hanging from trees
After bowing to our knees
Rhythmically vibrating human leaves
And with a cut
Their idea of our manhood lying at our feet
It's legal lynching
This racist death penalty

Freestylin'

Pieces of an excellent time
Ancient ways
And patterns scattered from the century of six
Has left me hanging
Back up against the upside red cliffs of the world
Daggers stained with crime
From then and my time
Who would have thought that beyond the brine
Across land I would stand
In a valley barbed wire
Away from the faint memories of the streets
Chaotic
The concrete jungle
Bob's "Rat Race" helps me keep the pace
And prayers for all times
Because the chalky red cliffs are my present reality
Only Ahad can save me now
Maybe when I look at it lying down I'll realize
Death becomes different
It is where justice
Where just I
Tested
Will come to know the fruits of my journey

Yusef A. Salaam #95A11..
Clinton Correctional Facility
P.O. Box 2001
Dannemora, N.Y. 12929-200

— on front

k put
— w/ picture

As an exonerated African-American man and an influential transformational speaker, **Yusef Salaam** has traveled all around the United States and the Caribbean to deliver powerful lectures and facilitate insightful conversations as he continues to touch lives and raise important questions about race and class, the failings of our criminal justice system, legal protections for vulnerable juveniles, and basic human rights.

Of his many notable speaking engagements, Yusef has been honored or spoken at: American University; Amherst College; the Andrew Goodman Foundation; the Black Star Project; Brooklyn Technical High School; Calhoun School; Cardozo School of Law; the City College of New York; Columbia Law School; Eureka College; Harvard University; Howard University School of Law; the Illinois Innocence Project; Justice League NYC; the Legal Aid Society; Lehman College; Mercy College; University of Miami Law School; MIT; NAACP; National Action Network; National Conference for Race & Ethnicity in American Higher Education; New Canaan Country School; The New School; New York University; Pace University; Penn State University; Rowan University; Smith College; Stony Brook University; TEDxSingSing; Towson University; Tulane University; the United Nations; the University of the Virgin Islands; University of Chicago, and many others.

Since his release more than 14 years ago, Yusef Salaam has become a devoted husband and father, poet, activist and inspirational speaker. He has committed himself to advocating for and educating people on the issues of mass incarceration, police brutality and misconduct, false confessions, press ethics and bias, race and law, and the disparities in America's criminal justice system – especially for young men of color.

His most recent awards have included a *Lifetime Achievement Award* from President Barack Obama (2016), an honorary *Doctorate of Humanities* from Anointed by God Ministries Alliance & Seminary (2014), and a long list of Proclamations – most notably from the New York City Council (2013).

YUSEF SPEAKS
Yusef Salaam

Leader • Motivator • Thinker

bookings@yusefspeaks.com
yusef@yusefspeaks.com

"Because the World Must Know"

- (f) YusefAbdusSalaam
- (🐦) yusefsalaam
- (📷) yusefsalaam
- (in) Yusef Salaam

www.YusefSpeaks.com